A Bear in War

Stephanie Innes &
Harry Endrulat

ILLUSTRATED BY Brian Deines

pajamapress

www.pajamapress.ca   info@pajamapress.ca

The publisher gratefully acknowledges the support of the Canada Council for the Arts and the Ontario Arts Council for its publishing program. We acknowledge the financial support of the Government of Canada through the Canada Book Fund (CBF) for our publishing activities.

Library and Archives Canada Cataloguing in Publication

Title: A bear in war / Stephanie Innes & Harry Endrulat ; illustrated by Brian Deines.
Names: Innes, Stephanie, author. | Endrulat, Harry, author. | Deines, Brian, illustrator.
Description: First edition. | Previously published: Toronto, Ontario, Canada: Pajama Press, 2012.
Identifiers: Canadiana 20190080310 | ISBN 9781772780864 (softcover)
Subjects: LCSH: World War, 1914-1918—Juvenile literature. | LCSH: Soldiers—Canada—Juvenile literature. | LCSH: Teddy bears—Juvenile literature. | LCSH: Father and child—Juvenile literature.
Classification: LCC D522.7 .I55 2012 | DDC j940.3—dc23

Publisher Cataloging-in-Publication Data (U.S.)

Names: Endrulat, Harry, author. | Innes, Stephanie, author. | Deines, Brian, illustrator.
Title: A Bear in War / authors Harry Endrulat and Stephanie Innes; illustrator Brian Deines.
Description: Toronto, Ontario Canada : Pajama Press, 2019. | Summary: "During World War One, a young girl slips her teddy bear into a care package for her father, a medic posted to the trenches of France. Although her father dies in the battle of Passchendaele, his belongings are shipped back to his family, along with the toy bear, which today sits in the Canadian War Museum in Ottawa"— Provided by publisher.
Identifiers: ISBN 978-1-77278-086-4 (paperback)
Subjects: LCSH: Teddy bears – Juvenile literature. | World War, 1914-1918 – Juvenile literature. | Parents—Death – Juvenile literature. | War memorials – Canada – Juvenile literature. | BISAC: JUVENILE NONFICTION / Biography and Autobiography / Literary. | JUVENILE NONFICTION / Historical / Military & Wars.
Classification: LCC D522.7E538Be |DDC 940.3 – dc23

Original art created with oil paint on canvas
Cover and book design by Martin Gould / martingould.com

Manufactured by Qualibre Inc. / Printplus
Printed in China

Pajama Press Inc.
181 Carlaw Ave., Suite 251, Toronto, Ontario, Canada M4M 2S1

Distributed in Canada by UTP Distribution
5201 Dufferin Street, Toronto, Ontario, Canada M3H 5T8

Distributed in the U.S. by Ingram Publisher Services
1 Ingram Blvd., La Vergne, TN 37086, USA

Facing page: (left) Aileen Rogers feeding chickens on the family farm; (right) A button from the uniform of Lieutenant Lawrence Browning Rogers.

In memory of the Rogers family – Lawrence, May, Howard, Aileen, Teddy – and all those whose lives were changed by war.

For my mother, Roberta Rogers Innes–S.I.

For Cathy, Harrison and Hayley – my inspiration–H.E.

For Dad and Sharon–B.D.

My favourite day began with a ride on a sleigh.

A girl with warm blue eyes held me tight as her mother guided the horses through the snow. We were bundled in a thick buffalo blanket to keep out the cold.

They were taking me to my new home in East Farnham, Quebec.

When the girl spoke, her breath made puffs of white. "My name is Aileen. What's yours?" she whispered as we glided along.

"Teddy," I said.

"It's nice to meet you, Teddy. I'm sure we're going to be best friends."

Aileen and Howard snowshoeing in East Farnham.

For the rest of the ride I sat quietly as we passed ice-tipped trees and frozen fields.

Finally, we reached a winding laneway that led to an old brick farmhouse.

Aileen helped her mother put the sleigh in the barn and unhitch the horses. I noticed she limped and wore a metal brace on her left leg.

Aileen took me inside her home. As we sat down near the wood-burning stove, she told me a secret.

"I can't walk, run or jump like the other children," she said. "I had a disease called polio. That's why I wear a brace on my leg."

I told Aileen a secret: "That makes no difference to me."

Mother started supper and made us some hot milk to drink.

"A little something to warm your spirits," she said.

Janet May Weaver Rogers and
Lawrence Browning Rogers.

Aileen's daddy and younger brother, Howard, came to meet me.

"He's kind of small, isn't he?" said Howard. I puffed out my chest to try to look bigger.

Daddy picked me up. "Sometimes the smallest ones have the biggest hearts," he said.

Daddy gave me back to Aileen. "Best to teach him about chores. We all have to do our share."

Chores were jobs we had to do. While Mother cooked, Howard and Daddy fetched wood for the stove. Aileen and I set the table.

Once supper was ready, we all sat down together. Father said a quick prayer of thanks and the family ate.

Lawrence in East Farnham, before leaving for World War I.

After supper, there were more chores. Aileen and I washed the dishes and Howard dried them. Then Father lit a lantern and we followed him into the barn.

Howard helped Daddy milk the cow. Aileen and Mother fed the horses hay and oats.

"The horses like sugar cubes, too," whispered Aileen. "But there are hardly any to buy since the war started."

"What's war?" I asked.

Aileen thought for a moment. "It's when people from one country fight people from another country."

"I don't like war," I said.

"Me neither," said Aileen.

Once the chores were done, we went back into the house. Mother sat in her rocking chair and crocheted a little red hat for me to wear to bed. Aileen and Howard played cards.

I sat with Daddy while he read the Montreal *Gazette* newspaper. There were lots of stories about a "Great War." He seemed worried.

Before long, Aileen and Howard started to yawn.

"Up to bed," said Mother. "Can't have you falling asleep at church tomorrow."

Daddy gave Aileen and me a piggyback ride upstairs.

A clipping from the Montreal *Gazette*. Many families in East Farnham got their war news from the paper.

Mother heated some black metal triangles called irons. She wrapped them in newspapers and towels and put them in Aileen's bed to keep us warm.

Aileen and I hopped under the covers. I had on my new red hat and Aileen had on a pink one.

We folded our hands and Aileen said a prayer: "Watch over Mother, Daddy, Howard, Teddy and me. Amen."

Aileen was scared of the dark, so Daddy stayed a little longer to help us fall asleep. He told us a story about three bears and a young girl with golden hair. It was very funny.

The next morning, Aileen, Howard and I woke early. It was still dark! I was tired, but we had to gather eggs for breakfast. Although it was cold outside, I stayed snug in the pocket of Aileen's coat.

Inside the chicken coop, Aileen and Howard reached under the hens' bellies and pulled out eggs. They put them in a basket. The eggs were still warm.

Aileen pointed to one hen. "She's a clucker," Aileen whispered. "She'll peck you if you try and take her eggs. We'll leave her for Howard." I thought that was a good idea.

After gathering the eggs, we fed the chickens boiled potato peels. "We can't waste any food," Aileen explained.

In the afternoon, we got ready for church. Aileen put on a dress and I wore a suit. We took the sleigh to town, passing stores with pictures hung in their windows.

"Those are recruiting posters," said Aileen. "The Canadian Army wants more soldiers for the war."

We reached the church and went inside. It seemed very empty.

"Where are all the people?" I asked Aileen.

"Lots of daddies are fighting the war in a place called Europe, across the ocean," Aileen explained.

"I'm glad Daddy is home with us," I said.

A World War I recruiting poster. The posters put enormous pressure on young men to help the Canadian military in Europe.

After church, we went home and made snowmen. Aileen
and Howard pretended they were soldiers fighting in the war.
We built a cave in the snow and pretended it was our dugout.
We made large snowballs and pretended they were bombs.

I didn't like that part of the game.

One night, Daddy came into Aileen's room.

"I'm going to fight in the war," he said.

"But I don't want you to go," said Aileen.

"I know. I'd rather stay here, too. But I feel it's my duty to help the other soldiers," said Daddy. "They need help to win the war."

"I'm proud of you, Daddy," Aileen said, giving him a hug.

After Daddy left, Aileen told me a secret: "Teddy, I wish Daddy could stay home."

In late spring, Daddy took a train to Valcartier, near Quebec City. When he got there, he sent us postcards. Learning how to be a soldier made Daddy very tired. He had to go for long marches. He didn't get much to eat – just buttered bread. And at night, he had to share a tent with nine other men.

"I miss you every minute of the day," he wrote.

We missed him, too.

In June, Aileen took me on my first train ride to visit Daddy. Other children and their mothers were also on the train to Valcartier. Everyone brought picnic lunches and packages of stamps, soap, tea, candy and socks for the soldiers.

At the camp, we watched Daddy and other soldiers ride on horseback. They looked very important in their uniforms. Daddy could do a lot of tricks on his horse. He jumped over fences and once picked up a handkerchief with his hand while riding!

Lawrence Browning Rogers in uniform.

At the end of the day, Daddy walked us to the train station and we hugged goodbye.

"Keep safe," Aileen whispered to Daddy. We knew he would be leaving for Europe very soon.

As the train pulled away, Daddy stood on the platform waving. Aileen held me up to the window and we waved back.

"I wish Daddy could come home with us, Teddy," Aileen said. "I don't like the war."

When we arrived home, Mother gathered paper, a fountain pen, an inkwell and a stack of stamps. Every night after supper she wrote to Daddy. Aileen and Howard wrote Daddy letters, too.

They told Daddy about school. Howard said he liked arithmetic and numbers best. Aileen said she skipped with the other girls and sometimes forgot about her brace. They said they were learning how Canada was helping England in the war.

In the morning, Mother walked Aileen, Howard and me to school. We would stop at the post office to check for letters from Daddy.

Some days we didn't get any. Other days we received four or five at a time.

Handwritten report cards belonging to Aileen and Howard.

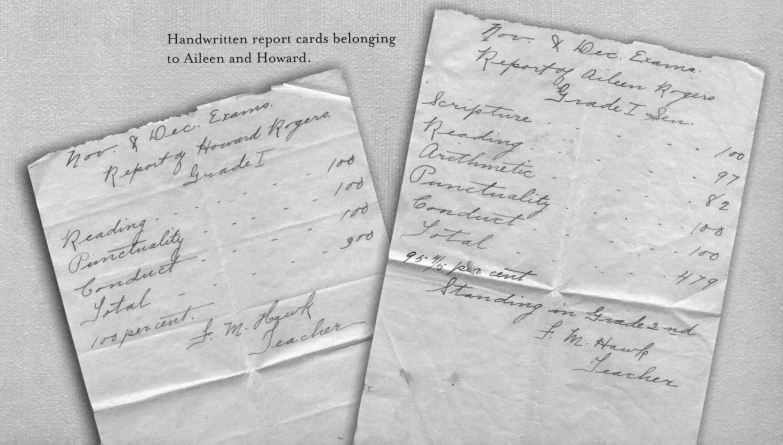

In one letter, Daddy told Mother he sailed to England on a big ship called the RMS *Hesperian*.

Daddy said the ship was very nice inside but that the waves made him feel sick. He even threw up while standing on guard.

But it wasn't all bad. One day, Daddy saw a school of porpoises jumping out of the ocean. I wished I could have seen that.

Daddy's boat landed in Portsmouth, England.

"I wish you had been with me," he wrote to us. "The water was full of war-ships and the sailors cheered us all the way in."

Daddy and the other soldiers took a train from Portsmouth to a place called Shorncliffe Camp.

There were lots of soldiers living there, waiting for their turn to go to the war.

"The countryside is beautiful," Daddy wrote. "Hedges divide the fields, which come right down to the water. Everything is so neat and orderly. This is a very pretty place but it is not home."

Christmas came and Daddy was still overseas. Mother said he was fighting in the trenches in a country called Belgium. In his letters he said he was cold and tired and missed us terribly.

"We need to send him something, Teddy," said Aileen. "Something to remind him of home and to keep him safe."

We thought for a long time. What should we send him? A book? A picture? Then, finally, we both had the same idea.

I would go to war.

Howard helped Aileen make a little bed for me out of a cardboard box. To keep me warm, they stuck a pair of wool socks inside. They wrapped the package in brown paper and punched holes in the box so I could breathe. Then they took me to the post office.

"Please take care of yourself and Daddy," Aileen said.

"I'll do my best," I said.

I travelled both by land and by sea. The journey was long and I lost track of time. Finally, someone tore open the box. It was Daddy!

"Teddy!" he said, squeezing me tight and smiling.

Daddy placed me in the front pocket of his army jacket and gave me a pat on the head.

"Well, my brave little bear, it's you and me now."

Daddy was now a medic in France. He liked helping the injured soldiers.

When the other soldiers seemed sad, Daddy cheered them up by telling them the war was almost over. Soon it would be time to go home.

He put bandages on the soldiers' cuts and made splints for their broken bones.

A lot of the time we sat in deep trenches. They were wet and cold – and there were rats everywhere. But the trenches helped protect us from bullets and bombs.

When a soldier got hurt, though, we would have to leave the trenches to help him. Sometimes we got hurt when a bomb exploded nearby. Sharp things would hit us.

Our bravery was noticed and we were given the Military Medal. Daddy pinned the medal to my chest and I wore it proudly.

The Military Medal awarded to Lieutenant Lawrence Browning Rogers for bravery.

Daddy and I thought about Mother, Howard and Aileen all the time.

On Christmas Eve, as we tried to stay dry and warm in the trenches, Daddy wrote a letter home:

"My stockings will be on my feet where they have been for the last seven days and where they will be for about eleven more. I will try and picture you and the kiddies hanging yours up and will perhaps see Santa Claus coming by on his way to you all and with hope that the stockings will get filled."

I continued to watch the war from Daddy's front pocket. I saw him help lots of soldiers.

That's what he was doing in the fall of 1917 at a battle called Passchendaele, when many soldiers died.

Daddy died that day, too, and I stayed in his pocket for a long, long time.

When the fighting finally stopped, a Canadian soldier found me tucked safely inside Daddy's pocket.

He sent me back to Canada with Daddy's uniform and medal.

Aileen was very surprised and happy to see me when she opened the package.

"Teddy, you came back!" Aileen said.

The report of Lieutenant Lawrence Browning Rogers' death from the Canadian government.

R.204-10M.
3364-25-7-1

List 52.

CIRCUMSTANCES OF DEATH REPORT.

DEPT
MILITIA & DEFENCE
FEB 23 1918
H.Q. CANADA

UNIT   5th Canadian Mounted Rifles.

NAME   ROGERS. Lawrence B.

RANK   Lieut.   NUMBER   ---

DATE OF DEATH   30-10 17.

CAUSE OF DEATH   Killed in action.

Detailed report of circumstances surrounding the death of this soldier.
(If "died of wounds" please report how wounds were received):-

The late Lieut.Rogers was instantly killed by enemy shell fire on October 30th 1917 while assisting in the Dressing of the wounded at forward R.A.P. during the attack on PASSCHENDAELE.

I was sad because Daddy was not with me. Aileen said she, Howard and Mother were very sad, too. She told me I was brave and that Daddy had received other medals.

That night Aileen told me another secret: "Daddy was a hero," she said. "He helped the soldiers who were hurt. I hope people always remember."

Three of Lieutenant Lawrence Browning Rogers' medals from World War I (from left to right): the 1914–1915 Star, the British War Medal, and the Victory Medal.

Daddy died many years ago, but I still try to keep his memory and the memories of the other fallen soldiers alive.

My home now is a glass case inside the Canadian War Museum.

Perhaps one day you can visit me. I'd be pleased to tell you my own secret – that I fought the war in the pocket of a hero.

The Canadian War Museum in Ottawa, Ontario, where Teddy now makes his home.

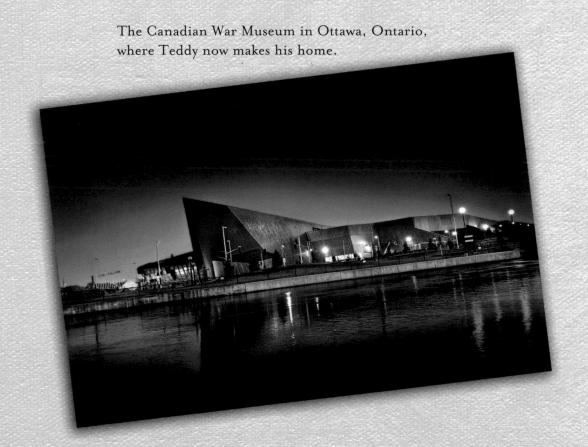

EPILOGUE

A Bear in War was inspired by the true story of "Teddy," a stuffed bear that was sent to the front lines during World War I.

Teddy belonged to ten-year-old Aileen Rogers, who lived with her family on a farm in East Farnham, Quebec. Her father, Lawrence Browning Rogers, enlisted in the Fifth Canadian Mounted Rifles at the age of thirty-six in 1915.

When Lawrence departed for training in Valcartier, Quebec, and then for the war, he left behind Aileen, seven-year-old Howard, and his wife, Janet May Weaver Rogers.

Janet and Lawrence exchanged more than two hundred letters during the two and a half years he was away. Aileen and Howard also wrote to Lawrence – and Aileen sent her beloved Teddy overseas to help protect him. However, it wasn't enough. On October 30, 1917, Lieutenant Lawrence Browning Rogers died at the battle of Passchendaele.

In 2002 Lawrence's granddaughter, Roberta Rogers Innes, found Teddy, the letters and other war memorabilia inside a large family briefcase. As she delved deeper, Roberta discovered how a Canadian family's strength was tested during the First World War and how a tiny stuffed bear became an enduring memento of their love.

Teddy now sits in the Canadian War Museum in Ottawa, Canada.

Clockwise from top right:
Lieutenant Lawrence Browning Rogers;
Three World War I uniform buttons;
Janet with Aileen and Howard, shortly
after Lawrence's death.